Original title:
Almond Sparks Amid the Griffin Ledge

Copyright © 2025 Swan Charm
All rights reserved.

Author: Sebastian Sarapuu
ISBN HARDBACK: 978-1-80562-021-1
ISBN PAPERBACK: 978-1-80563-542-0

Chronicles of Magic Above the Fog

Above the fog, the moonlight glows,
Whispers of magic, where the wind blows.
Trees dance gently, their shadows play,
In a world of wonder, night turns to day.

Secrets are hidden in every breeze,
Woven spells linger among the trees.
A creature stirs in the cool, soft night,
With eyes like lanterns, sparkling bright.

The river sings tales of ages gone,
Of wizards and spells cast upon the dawn.
As stars twinkle in a velvet sea,
In this realm of magic, wild and free.

In misty valleys, echoes call,
Adventures await beneath ancient pall.
Through tangled paths where shadows roam,
Magic awaits, calling you home.

So take a step, let your heart soar,
Dance in the twilight, ask for more.
For up in the sky, where dreams entwine,
Chronicles of magic, forever shine.

A Breadth of Wild Wishes on the Highside

On the highside, wishes take flight,
Carried on breezes, sparkling bright.
They flutter and dance like leaves in the air,
Whispering secrets without a care.

Children's laughter echoes with glee,
As wild wishes weave through the trees.
Each wish a feather, so light, so free,
Floating on dreams like a ship on the sea.

In twilight's glow, the sky ablaze,
A tapestry woven in magical ways.
Each star a wish, a hope shining clear,
Guiding lost hearts, drawing them near.

The mountains stand tall, a guardians' might,
Holding the wishes that dance in the night.
For in every moment, a story awaits,
A breath of wild wishes that destiny creates.

So cast your dreams in the warm evening glow,
Let them soar high where only they know.
For on the highside, where wishes align,
A world of enchantment forever shall shine.

The Pulse of Nature in Wandering Hearts

In the forest, whispers blend,
Tales of old begin to wend.
Leaves that dance in gentle glee,
Secrets kept from you and me.

Mossy stones and winding trails,
Tell of dreams where hope never fails.
Each step treads a sacred path,
Where silence sings in nature's math.

Breezes carry laughter bright,
Sunset paints the sky in light.
Starlit skies, a guiding muse,
In wandering hearts, love will choose.

Through the glades, a magic weaves,
Nature's pulse, an echo leaves.
In the stillness, stories grow,
A timeless bond with all we know.

Luminous Insights from Above the Abyss

In the dark, a flicker glows,
Truth emerges as it flows.
A spark of wisdom, fierce and bright,
Guiding souls through endless night.

Stars like lanterns in the void,
Fading doubts and fears destroyed.
With each gleam, a hint of grace,
Revealing life's enchanted face.

Voices whisper from the deep,
Secrets ancient, secrets keep.
Above the abyss, spirits soar,
Luminous insights, forevermore.

Fear and hope in balance dance,
Fate reveals its boldest chance.
In the void, we find our truth,
Shining bright in timeless youth.

Enigma of Urgency and Calm Whispers

The clock ticks loud, a race to run,
Yet in the chaos, peace is spun.
Urgency breathes in every heart,
While calm whispers play their part.

In the tempest, find your core,
Amid the storm, there lies the shore.
A gentle touch, a guiding hand,
Where silence speaks, and understands.

Moments fleeting, like the breeze,
Yet in stillness, we find ease.
Feel the pulse of time and fate,
In every choice, we navigate.

Between the rush and quiet sighs,
In whispers soft, the truth lies.
An enigma of our days,
Life's complexity in endless ways.

The Charisma of the Highside Realm

In heights where dreams are spun to gold,
A realm of wonders, bold and old.
Mountains whisper tales of years,
Echoing through both joy and tears.

In the clouds, we touch the sky,
Where every venture dares to fly.
Stars like jewels grace the night,
Magnifying the heart's delight.

With every summit, courage grows,
In heights unknown, the spirit flows.
The charisma of this place is clear,
Where every heartbeat sings to cheer.

Let the winds carry your dreams,
Through valleys bright and moonlit beams.
In the highs, we learn to strive,
Embracing the magic to feel alive.

Whispers of the Starlit Grove

In the hush of night's embrace,
Where starlight weaves its gentle lace,
Soft whispers drift on the cool night air,
Secrets hidden with tender care.

The ancient trees stand tall and wise,
Beneath the glow of shimmering skies,
Their branches sway with stories old,
Of dreams and laughter, soft and bold.

Moonbeams dance on the silken grass,
In the grove where shadows pass,
A symphony of silence sings,
As magic stirs on silver wings.

Fireflies flicker like tiny stars,
While echoing softly, the night's guitars,
A melody of the heart's delight,
In this grove where dreams take flight.

With every step, a tale unfolds,
In whispered tones, the night beholds,
The secrets shared by night's embrace,
In the starlit grove, a sacred space.

Echoes of Wings in Dappled Light

In the glade where sunlight streams,
Softly weaving through golden dreams,
Wings whisper tales of yesteryears,
Echoes born of laughter and tears.

Dappled light on the forest floor,
Invites the heart to seek for more,
While breezes hum a gentle tune,
Beneath the watching, timeless moon.

Birds take flight, their shadows blend,
In a game where time won't bend,
With every flutter, a story spins,
In the dance of where magic begins.

The leaves above converse in sighs,
Sharing secrets with the skies,
Nature's chorus, soft and bright,
Echoes of wings in dappled light.

Each moment captured, forever clear,
In the heart of those who dare appear,
For in this realm of serenity,
Awaits the gift of divinity.

The Myth of the Golden Orchard

In a realm where secrets lie,
Beneath the wide and open sky,
Grows an orchard, lush and rare,
Golden fruits hanging in midair.

Whispers tell of dreams unreal,
Of tastes that time cannot conceal,
With every bite, a wish takes flight,
In the magic of the endless night.

Twilit shadows dance on boughs,
As the evening softly bows,
To the stars that twinkle and gleam,
In the orchard of a wishful dream.

From branches low to the heavens high,
It beckons all with a friendly sigh,
Promises kept in golden glow,
The myth of the orchard, a tale to sow.

So wander forth where wonders reign,
And cherish the fruits of joy and pain,
For in each bite, the heart will soar,
In the golden orchard forevermore.

Shadows Play Among Jewel Leaves

In the forest where colors collide,
Shadows play with the stars as guide,
Among the leaves like jewels they shine,
Reflecting tales of the divine.

Emerald glimmers, ruby glows,
As the softest breeze gently flows,
Each leaf a canvas, a story spun,
With whispers told when day is done.

A dance of light, a chase of dreams,
Where magic flows in gentle streams,
The shadows waltz in playful guise,
Beneath the gaze of watchful skies.

In this realm of vibrant hues,
Nature hums her ancient blues,
While shadows weave their mysteries deep,
Among the leaves, where secrets sleep.

So come, behold this enchanting scene,
Where shadows and jewels will intervene,
In the dance of dusk, where spirits weave,
The magic found among the leaves.

Flickers of Flame Beneath the Nest

In shadows deep, a spark does glow,
The whispers stir as night winds blow.
A nest of dreams in twilight's embrace,
Flickers of flame in a hidden place.

The stars above twinkle and tease,
Guardians watching with gentle ease.
Each ember dances, a story to tell,
Of warmth and light in a dreamy swell.

Feathers rustle, secrets unfold,
A tapestry woven of legends old.
Beneath the nest where hopes ignite,
Flickers of flame in the heart of night.

With every breath, the fire exhales,
A chorus of magic in soft, sweet trails.
The world awakens, enchanted, alive,
In the warmth of the flames, the spirits thrive.

So gather close, let the glow unite,
In the flickers of flame, we find our light.
Together we'll journey, hand in hand,
Beneath the nest, in this enchanted land.

Dance of the Celestial Beasts

Under the moon, the wild ones prance,
A waltz of light, a cosmic dance.
With silver fur and eyes like stars,
They twirl in beauty, near and far.

The night sky whispers secrets sweet,
As constellations guide their feet.
Each creature swirling in mystic grace,
A ballet woven through time and space.

From forest depths to mountains high,
The beasts unite, their spirits fly.
With every leap, they paint the air,
In colors bright, beyond compare.

The drumming hearts of nature's song
Echo in pulses, enduring and strong.
In this celestial symphony, we see,
The world alive in harmony.

So watch the dance, let your soul take flight,
In the embrace of this endless night.
For in this moment, we all belong,
In the dance of beasts, we sing along.

Embers in the Enchanted Glade

Beneath the boughs where shadows play,
Whispers of magic weave and sway.
Embers flicker in the twilight haze,
A spark ignites in the evening's gaze.

The fairies gather, their laughter bright,
Dancing around the gentle light.
With every twinkle, the glade comes alive,
In the warmth of the embers, dreams survive.

Moonbeams filter through the leaves,
As the night enchants, and the heart believes.
Each glow a promise, a wish to hold,
In the enchanted woods, stories unfold.

Soft melodies flow from the stream,
In the presence of magic, we dare to dream.
Embers whisper of times long past,
In the glade where the spell is cast.

As dawn approaches, the embers wane,
Yet in our hearts, their warmth remains.
For in this glade, where wonders reside,
The embers of magic will forever guide.

The Guardian's Glimmering Flight

Above the trees where shadows gleam,
The Guardian soars, a protector's dream.
Wings of silver grace the air,
With a shimmering trail that sparks the rare.

Through mists of time, in dawn's soft glow,
The Guardian's path is one we know.
With every beat, the heart takes flight,
A beacon of hope in the endless night.

In moments fleeting, the world stands still,
As magic awakens with strength and will.
A guardian's gaze, fierce and wise,
Guides the lost 'neath the vast, starry skies.

With whispers of ancient tales untold,
The guardian's spirit, courageous and bold.
In the sky's embrace, so vast and wide,
We find our peace in this noble guide.

So when you gaze at the moonlit flight,
Remember the guardian, a symbol of light.
In every shadow, their presence near,
A promise of safety, dispelling our fear.

Whispers of Amber Horizons

In the dusk where shadows loom,
Amber hues dispel the gloom.
Softly gliding, whispers call,
Echoing through the ancient hall.

Dreamers linger, eyes alight,
Chasing stars that grace the night.
Tales of old, like fireflies,
Dance beneath the velvet skies.

Upon the hills where silence weaves,
Every rustle tells of leaves.
In twilight's arms, the world holds breath,
Caught between life and death.

With amber light, the moments freeze,
Caught in time like buzzing bees.
Dreams unfold, take shape and soar,
Forever seeking, ever more.

Whispers linger, soft and near,
Carried on winds, sweet and clear.
In the glow of amber's grace,
Find your heart in time and space.

Glimmers on the Stone Abyss

In the depths where darkness reigns,
Glimmers shine like hidden chains.
Stone by stone, the whispers tread,
Guiding hearts where none have fled.

Secrets murmur, dreams entwine,
Through the shadows, soft they shine.
A dance of light, a spark of hope,
Entwined in the abyss's scope.

Beneath the weight of ancient night,
Flickers pause, a fleeting sight.
Leaping forth like stars on high,
Challenging the deepened sky.

In the cavern where echoes dwell,
Hidden tales begin to swell.
Every glimmer, every spark,
Breaks the silence, cleaves the dark.

For in the stone, the magic sleeps,
Awaits the light, the heart that leaps.
Forever marked by time's embrace,
Each glimmer holds a sacred place.

Echoes of Myth and Nutmeg

Through the air, sweet nutmeg swirls,
Echoes of tales from forgotten worlds.
Fables spun in twilight's glow,
Where mysteries of magic flow.

A gentle breeze, a haunting tune,
Weaving threads beneath the moon.
In the heart of the forest vast,
The heartbeat of legends past.

Whispers of knights and beasts of yore,
In every leaf, a tale to explore.
Nutmeg's scent, a potion rare,
Unraveling dreams woven in air.

Where children play and shadows dance,
In this realm, give fate a chance.
Echoes weave through branches wide,
A tapestry where dreams reside.

From dawn till dusk, the stories play,
In nutmeg whispers, they find their way.
Embrace the myths that softly call,
For in their echo, we find it all.

Flickers of Twilight over Crags

When twilight drapes the rugged crags,
Flickers of light, the day's last rags.
Softly painted in hues of fire,
As day retreats, dreams inspire.

Mountains stand with shadows cast,
Echoes of whispers from the past.
Each flicker holds a secret tight,
Beneath the watchful, starry night.

Gentle winds on rocky trails,
Carry the scent of ancient tales.
Twilight dances on the stone,
In nature's arms, the heart finds home.

From peaks so high, the world seems small,
Flickers beckon, calling all.
Hearts that wander, souls that roam,
Find in twilight, a sacred home.

Glimmers spark within the dark,
Nurtured in the evening's arc.
As crags embrace the fleeting light,
Wonders bloom in the arms of night.

Fireflies over Celestial Columns

Amid the night, a gentle glow,
Fireflies dance, putting on a show,
Their lights twinkle in the dusky veil,
Guiding dreams on a mystic trail.

Beneath the stars, the columns rise,
Touching realms where magic lies,
Each flicker whispers tales of yore,
Of ancient paths and hidden lore.

Through shadowed woods, they weave and play,
Inviting wanderers to stay,
In this embrace of twilight's hue,
Where wonders bloom and hearts renew.

With every flutter, secrets spun,
A tapestry of night begun,
Emerald glades, their refuge found,
As whispers of the night surround.

So let them lead, these lights so bright,
Into the realm of pure delight,
Where joy and magic intertwine,
In dancing paths of the divine.

Reverberations of Hallowed Heights

Echoes rise in morning's breath,
Awakening to life's caress,
The mountains hum a sacred tune,
Drawing hearts beneath the moon.

From hallowed heights, the world expands,
Creation's pulse in gentle hands,
Spirits soar on winds of grace,
Time stands still in this embrace.

Each stone has tales of joy and woe,
Of travelers who dared to go,
With every step, an age they tread,
With whispered hope, their fears they shed.

Beneath the sky, the sun will shine,
Painting dreams on earth's design,
In vibrant hues, the echoes sing,
Of hallowed heights and what they bring.

Let echoes guide the souls who seek,
The whispered words of the meek,
For in the heights, we find our way,
Where love and light forever stay.

Serengeti Shadows in a Distant Realm

In shadows deep where whispers roam,
The Serengeti calls us home,
Underneath a vast, star-lit sea,
Where wild hearts dance, forever free.

Golden grasses sway and twine,
In ancient rhythms, nature's design,
The moon casts dreams on the quiet ground,
With every pulse, magic is found.

From whispers soft, a lion's roar,
Echoes through the mythic lore,
Each footfall tells of journeys grand,
In this enchanted, timeless land.

A canvas painted in dusk's embrace,
Where shadows linger, and spirits race,
In every glance, a tale unfolds,
Of courage bold and love untold.

And as we wander through this night,
With hearts aflame, our souls take flight,
In the realm where shadows play,
Forever lost, yet found, we stay.

Candy Floss Clouds over Rugged Peaks

Softly curling, clouds like dreams,
Candy floss in sunlight beams,
Over rugged peaks, they float and sway,
Painting skies where wishes play.

Whispers sweet on a gentle breeze,
Time stands still beneath the trees,
Adventure calls, a siren's song,
Inviting hearts where they belong.

In valleys rich where shadows run,
The world awakens, day begun,
Each mountain high, a daring quest,
As candy clouds embrace the rest.

With every step, we chase the light,
Through meadows bright, our spirits ignite,
In laughter, joy, we find our way,
On this magical, sunlit day.

So let the sweets of life bestow,
A taste of dreams, a wondrous glow,
Where rugged peaks meet love's embrace,
In candy clouds of timeless grace.

When Light Meets the Ancient Stone

In shadows deep where whispers dwell,
A flicker glows, a distant bell.
The stone holds tales of times long past,
In silence frozen, shadows cast.

With every ray that breaks the night,
The ancient rocks begin to light.
A dance of memories intertwines,
Where dreams of yore the heart defines.

The echoes of a bygone age,
In every crack, a written page.
As twilight bends, the stories breathe,
Their secrets rise, like mist beneath.

A symphony of light and stone,
In every hue, the past, we own.
The warmth of sun on weathered ground,
A timeless bond, forever found.

The Flickering Hope on Celestial Ventures

Beyond the stars where shadows play,
A flickering hope can find its way.
In darkness deep, the heart ignites,
A beacon bright on endless nights.

Each twinkling light a whispered dream,
A tapestry of thoughts that beam.
The vast expanse, a canvas wide,
Where hopes and fears in silence bide.

In every pulse, a story wakes,
A myriad of paths it takes.
Through cosmic storms and asteroids' dance,
The heart holds tight to every chance.

With every star, a wish unspun,
A flicker bold, a race begun.
In celestial realms where wonders gleam,
The flickering hope, our guiding beam.

A Spark of Color in Silent Spaces

In quiet nooks where shadows twine,
A spark of color starts to shine.
Beneath the veil of muted grace,
Life's vivid strokes begin to trace.

The canvas waits with bated breath,
To dance with hues that cheat at death.
A blush of scarlet, a dash of gold,
In silent spaces, stories told.

Each stroke a heartbeat, soft and true,
The vibrant whispers break right through.
In every shade, a tale unwinds,
In silent spaces, hope finds binds.

With every twinkle, dreams ignite,
A spark of color paints the night.
In quiet places, joys collide,
With every stroke, the soul's bright guide.

Ascending Luminescence on Broad Peaks

On towering heights where eagles soar,
Ascend the skies, a lustrous roar.
The sun breaks free, the day awakes,
In blazing hues, the silence shakes.

Each peak aglow with golden light,
A dance of flames in morning's sight.
In every corner, shadows flee,
As nature hums its melody.

The world unfurls, a vibrant expanse,
Where colors blend in bold romance.
From granite walls to skies so wide,
The luminescence cannot hide.

With every step upon the crest,
A sense of peace, a heartbeat blessed.
Ascending high, we touch the sun,
In broad peaks' glow, our hearts become one.

Flashes of Magic on Terraced Shelves

In gardens where secrets softly hum,
Colors of whimsy quietly come.
Whispers of spells weave through the air,
Guiding the heart to memories rare.

Beneath the moon's watch, shadows will dance,
Each flicker of light sparks a chance.
With laughter carried on breezy sighs,
Wonder unfolds beneath starlit skies.

Moss-covered stones tell stories untold,
Of dreams that shimmer in threads of gold.
Branches sway gently, a melody played,
In this enchanted glen where hopes are laid.

The nightingale sings, with joy it has known,
In every note, a magic has grown.
Through terraced paths where fairies weave,
A tapestry spun for those who believe.

Mystic Flare of Creatures Above

In twilight's embrace, the skies ignite,
With flares of wonders, a brilliant sight.
Creatures aloft in a waltz of delight,
They serenade stars in their dazzling flight.

Glimmers of wisdom, the owls call forth,
Guiding lost souls who wander the north.
With feathers of night cloaked in shadows deep,
They watch over dreams as the world drifts to sleep.

Shooting stars scatter like whispers of fate,
As pixies and sprites weave their threads of create.
The moonbeam's glow shines on wings made of light,
In this realm where the magic takes flight.

Mysterious figures in the deep azure,
Flutter and flit, their spirits so pure.
With each twinkle, a tale unfolds wide,
In the mystic flare where old legends abide.

Glance of Light on Nature's Canvas

Upon the brook, the sun's fingers play,
Awakening colors that dance and sway.
Petals burst forth, a palette anew,
Nature's canvas, where dreams come true.

Golden rays brush the leaves with a smile,
Creating a masterpiece, pure and versatile.
The breeze carries scents of flourishing life,
In harmony spun, as the sirens of strife.

Mountains stand guard with majesty grand,
Holding tight stories of seasons unplanned.
Each glance of light, a brush of the past,
Painting the world, where memories last.

Rivers flow gently, reflections of peace,
As whispers of wonder never cease.
On this vibrant stage where silence resounds,
A glance of light is where magic abounds.

The Embers of Glee on Rugged Edges

At dawn's first light on the rugged brink,
The embers of glee begin to wink.
Heat of excitement ignites the air,
In every crack, a story to share.

Boulders stand firm, holding tales so old,
Of hearts emboldened and spirits that bold.
With every heartbeat, the wilderness sings,
Of laughter and joy that adventure brings.

Echoes of footsteps on trails made of stone,
Once ventured by wanderers, never alone.
One can feel magic in the breeze that swirls,
Where nature's embrace unfurls and twirls.

As shadows stretch long, day begins to slow,
The embers of glee in sunsets aglow.
Amidst rugged edges, where dreams freely roam,
A sanctuary found, forever a home.

Light Play on the Gabled Rocks

Sunlight dances on pointed peaks,
Casting shadows where silence speaks.
Crimson crests in the morning glow,
Awakening tales of long ago.

Whispers of breezes through emerald leaves,
Carrying stories, the heart believes.
Gabled rocks stand proud and tall,
Guardians of dreams that never fall.

Clouds drift softly as laughter swells,
Nature weaves magic with its spells.
Each stone a keeper of ancient lore,
Echoing secrets forevermore.

Dappled light through the branches weaves,
An ethereal portrait that never leaves.
On the gables, the light will play,
In the enchantment of a stunning display.

Fragments of Stardust on Turquoise

Beneath the sky, a turquoise sea,
Fragments of stardust twinkle free.
Glistening grains where whispers lie,
Dancing dreams in the night sky.

Crimson shells held by the tide,
Stories of sailors who never died.
Ripples of time in each tiny piece,
Carrying wonders that never cease.

With each wave, a promise is cast,
Echoes of futures and tales from the past.
The moonlight softens the ocean's sigh,
As stardust flickers in the azure sky.

In hidden coves where treasures sleep,
The secrets of galaxies gently creep.
Nature's palette, alive with grace,
A mosaic of dreams in this sacred space.

Secrets Beneath the Ancient Wing

In twilight's hush, the shadows grow,
Ancient wings in soft winds blow.
Secrets lie in the forest deep,
In whispers of magic, the world will weep.

Under each feather, a journey hides,
Wisdom collected where time abides.
Glimmers of truth in the dark and light,
Revealing tales of forgotten flight.

Beneath old branches, lost hearts find,
The pulse of nature, tender and kind.
A tapestry woven with threads of fate,
Each secret a marker, a wondrous gate.

With every flutter, the echoes sing,
Carrying promises on wonder's wing.
Boundless lore in the stillness holds,
Treasures of ages, forever unfolds.

Shimmering Whispers in Midsummer Twilight

As day bows down to the night's embrace,
Shimmering whispers through time and space.
Midsummer twilight brings dreams alive,
Where shadows and light together thrive.

Fireflies dance in a waltz so bright,
Guiding lost souls through the velvety night.
Soft silver beams on dewy grass,
Echoing moments that fleetingly pass.

In the hush, the world holds its breath,
Cradled by night as the stars bequeath.
Stories woven with delicate care,
Whispers of magic, lingering in air.

A serenade sung by crickets near,
Filling the silence with songs we hear.
Midsummer twilight, a timeless art,
Painting the dusk on a dreaming heart.

Sparks of Creation on High Rock

Upon the peak where shadows loom,
Stars ignite, dispelling gloom.
Whispers of the ancient days,
Dance with light in mystic ways.

Crafted dreams in glowing threads,
Twilight glimmers where hope treads.
Each flicker tells a tale anew,
Of boundless skies, of wishing's hue.

A spark released from time's embrace,
Illuminates the endless space.
Children of the cosmos sing,
Of life, and joy, and everything.

Let hearts ignite, let spirits soar,
With every flash, forevermore.
For on this rock where wonders play,
Creation breathes a bright ballet.

In unity, we find our mark,
As souls unite, we leave our spark.
Each heartbeat echoes, loud and clear,
In the high realm, we hold so dear.

Celestial Caresses on Dusty Paths

Beneath the arch of night so vast,
We wander trails of dreams amassed.
Celestial fingers trace the ground,
In whispered silence, magic found.

Distant stars become our guide,
On these dusty paths, we glide.
With stardust kissing every stone,
We tread upon the unknown.

Moonlight bathes the world in grace,
Every step, a gentle embrace.
Harmony sings in the soft air,
Chasing shadows, light so rare.

A celestial breeze lifts our hearts,
Unraveling the thread of parts.
With every sigh, the cosmos bends,
As time dissolves and love transcends.

Journey onward, hand in hand,
Exploring every dream-touched land.
For in each glide, a moment stays,
Marked forever in starry ways.

Enchanted Zest of Distant Glades

In glades where sunlight softly beams,
Nature weaves her vibrant dreams.
With every leaf a story told,
Of whispered wishes, brave and bold.

The air, alive with fragrant zest,
Wraps our spirits in a nest.
Bubbling brooks and laughing vines,
Create a realm where love entwines.

Dancing shadows, twirling leaves,
In this place, the heart believes.
Each rustle sings of hidden spells,
Where the ancient magic dwells.

Crickets chirp a lullaby,
While fireflies light the twilight sky.
Every moment, beauty flows,
As the enchanted glade bestows.

Let us linger under boughs,
Make a promise, craft our vows.
In the zest of life's embrace,
Finding joy in nature's grace.

Luminous Echoes against Stone and Sky

In the valley where echoes play,
Stones remember the light of day.
With every beat, their voices blend,
In harmony that shall not end.

Echoes rise from deep within,
Telling tales of loss and win.
Against the sky, they weave and swirl,
In a dance, the stories twirl.

Luminous lights on stony heights,
Paint the canvas of countless nights.
Whispers of ancient souls awake,
Carving paths that stars can take.

Each note a thread connecting time,
In the tapestry of heart and rhyme.
Resonate through earth and air,
As echoes linger everywhere.

Let us listen to the call,
Of shimmering lives both great and small.
For in each echo, a truth shall show,
The light we seek, the love we know.

The Serenade of Winged Elders

In twilight's hush, their shadows glide,
Familiar whispers, where secrets reside.
With wings that shimmer, tales they weave,
A serenade for those who believe.

Through azure skies, they soar and dance,
Guardians of dreams, in a timeless trance.
With every flutter and distant call,
They weave their magic, enchanting all.

From age-old oaks, their songs arise,
Echoing softly 'neath starlit skies.
Elders of wisdom, they share their grace,
Spreading joy through the vastness of space.

In emerald leaves, their laughter springs,
As moonlight glistens on delicate wings.
Together they twirl in a ballet of light,
Painting the darkness with colors so bright.

With the dawn's embrace, they take their flight,
Fading like dreams into morning's light.
Yet in our hearts, their songs remain,
The serenade of winged elders, a gentle refrain.

Echoed Laughter by Perched Heights

High on the ridge, where the wild winds sway,
Echoed laughter ignites the day.
With every gust, the trees respond,
Nature's laughter, a bond so fond.

The sun spills gold on the sprawling view,
Birds chirp merrily, their joy anew.
Above the world, in their lofty nest,
They share their secrets, a playful jest.

Clouds drift lazily, shadows they cast,
Reminders of moments, both fleeting and vast.
Among the heights, where the breezes play,
Echoed laughter fills the soft ballet.

Every branch sways to a whimsical tune,
Under the watch of the silver moon.
With hearts unburdened, free from all ties,
They celebrate life in the open skies.

Through whispers of leaves, their mirth ascends,
In the gentle breeze, where joy never ends.
Each note a promise, each giggle a flight,
In the echoes of laughter, all is right.

Captured Breath of the Nature's Watch

In the forest's heart, where shadows play,
Nature's watch holds magic at bay.
Through rustling leaves, a breath is caught,
Moments untouched, in silence wrought.

Glimmers of sunlight through branches weave,
A tapestry splendid, for those who believe.
Each dew-kissed petal, a whisper clear,
The language of nature, for all to hear.

As rivers flow softly, time stands still,
The rhythm of life, a gentle thrill.
Captured breaths in the still of the trees,
Dance with the wind, carried with ease.

In twilight's embrace, the colors fade,
Yet still, the echoes of peace are laid.
A sigh of the earth, a moment divine,
In nature's lullaby, the stars align.

With every heartbeat, the wilds relate,
Tales of the ages, spun by fate.
In the stillness found, whispers alight,
Captured breaths guide us into the night.

Glows of Luminary Thoughts

In the quiet hours of the dark night,
Glows of luminary thoughts take flight.
Dreams unfurl like petals in bloom,
Chasing shadows that dance in their loom.

Beneath the stars, where wishes reside,
Thoughts like lanterns, they glow and glide.
Whispers of hope on the gentle breeze,
With every flicker, time seems to freeze.

As dawn's first light starts to appear,
The luminary thoughts remind us here,
In whispered moments, we find our way,
Guided by stars, through night into day.

Each sparkle a promise, each twinkle a sign,
In the tapestry of dreams, our spirits entwine.
For in the glow, we all can see,
The light within, setting our souls free.

In every heartbeat, in every sigh,
Luminary thoughts dance across the sky.
Radiant and bold, they light up the dark,
A symphony of hope, igniting a spark.

Chronicles of the Fire-Kissed Trees

In the heart of the glen, where the shadows play,
The trees hold secrets of a bygone day.
Their leaves blush red in the amber glow,
Winds whisper tales of the fallen snow.

Branches entwined, a tapestry spun,
Fires dance gently, revealing the fun.
The roots reach deep into ancient lore,
Time flows like rivers to an endless shore.

A spirit awakens in the twilight hour,
Guarding the whispers of nature's power.
Each crackle and spark is a voice in the night,
Binding the world in a radiant light.

With every gust, the embers lift high,
Chasing the shadows, they reach for the sky.
In silence, they bask, these fire-kissed trees,
Guardians of stories, carried by breeze.

Flickering Glories in Hidden Valleys

In valleys concealed, where the soft light falls,
Flickering glories echo through the walls.
Petals of starlight dance on the dew,
Each shimmer a promise of wonders anew.

Cascading whispers of flowers in bloom,
Unveiling the magic that banishes gloom.
A haven of colors, where dreams serenade,
Nature composing in bright, bold parade.

Moss carpets the stones, rich emerald threads,
While the breeze carries secrets, the heart gently treads.
The past and the present weave here as one,
In hidden valleys, where fortunes are spun.

With every heartbeat, the glories ignite,
Illuminating paths with their pastel light.
To wander through wonders, to cherish the grace,
Is to find in the valleys a magical place.

Radiance Between the Mountains' Grip

Between the great mountains, vast and austere,
Lies a secret of light that dances near.
Sunbeams break through with a gentle embrace,
Illuminating paths in a shimmered trace.

Crisp air carries stories of ages gone by,
Where echoes of laughter reach up to the sky.
Rivers weave silver through valleys of green,
In the radiance held where the sun has been.

Each stone has a memory, each trail has a song,
Of journeys yet taken, of where we belong.
Through meadows and shadows, the wildflowers sway,
In the arms of the mountains, forever they play.

The clouds whisper softly of tales untold,
Of bravery, magic, and legends of old.
And as the sun sets, under twilight's kiss,
The mountains stand watch, in their tranquil bliss.

The Tapestry of Light and Legend

In the loom of the cosmos, threads intertwine,
Crafting a tapestry, with tales divine.
Each stitch a memory, woven with care,
Revealing our truths, in the soft evening air.

Stars sparkle brightly, like gems in the night,
Guiding the lost with their flickering light.
Legends unfurl in the moon's gentle gaze,
Dancing like phantoms in ethereal haze.

Mist wraps the mountains, cloaking the past,
Whispers of heroes that shadows have cast.
In every heartbeat, we feel the embrace,
Of stories that linger, a magical space.

With colors of twilight, the canvas ignites,
A glorious spectrum of endless delights.
In the folds of the fabric, we dream and we dare,
For the tapestry shines with love everywhere.

Illumination in Shadowed Heights

In valleys deep where whispers dwell,
A shimmer wakes, a distant bell.
Through tangled roots and mossy ground,
The light of stars begins to sound.

A flicker bright, a haunting tune,
As shadows dance beneath the moon.
With every breath, the night unfolds,
A tapestry of dreams retold.

In secret nooks where fears reside,
Courage blooms, a steady guide.
The mountains hum with tales of yore,
Of those who dared, and sought for more.

Above the peaks, where falcons soar,
The spell of night invites us more.
With every glance at skies adorned,
We find the light, a spark reborn.

Beyond the ridges, silent skies,
A flicker moves, a sweet surprise.
Illumination weaves its art,
As shadows whisper to the heart.

Dances with Celestial Seeds

In gardens lush where stardust falls,
The earth receives the night's soft calls.
Among the blooms, the secrets play,
As dreams entwine in soft array.

With every breeze, the petals sway,
Where wishes float like clouds of gray.
In whispered tones, they plant their plea,
To dance with seeds of destiny.

A gentle hand, a loving touch,
Each breath of life means all so much.
The cosmos spins, we're part of it,
Where silent hopes and magic sit.

Beneath the moon's ethereal glow,
The seeds of light begin to grow.
With fervent grace, we chance our fate,
To weave the dreams that time creates.

Around the world, the stories weave,
In colors bright, the heart believes.
To dance with seeds beneath the night,
Is to embrace the cosmic light.

Radiance Beyond the Feathered Edge

At dawn's first blush, the world awakes,
With wings that flutter, silence breaks.
In shadows cast by feathery grace,
A spark ignites, time starts to race.

The sun ascends, a golden shield,
To every heart, its warmth revealed.
As creatures stir and nature sings,
We sense the joy that morning brings.

A dance of light on shimmered dew,
Where whispers tell what dreams pursue.
The feathered edge, a line divine,
Where wishes meld and spirits shine.

Each beam transformed in radiant glow,
Reminds us of the paths we sow.
With eager hearts, we chase the dawn,
To find the truths that linger on.

Beyond the skies, where hope takes flight,
We rise anew with each daylight.
Radiance awaits—an open door,
Inviting all who wish for more.

Quartz Dreams and Rustic Delights

In corners hushed, the treasures hide,
With quartz that glimmers, hope inside.
Each crystal holds a tale to tell,
Of rustic charms where memories dwell.

A wooden chair, a woven thread,
Where laughter weaves through words unsaid.
The scents of spice, the warmth of bread,
Invite us close, where dreams are fed.

Among the jars, the fruits of earth,
Evoke the magic, recall the mirth.
With every taste, a story found,
In rustic delights, our hearts resound.

The sunlight streams through glassy hues,
As shadows dance with morning dues.
Quartz dreams burst forth like morning rays,
Revealing love in subtle ways.

In simple things, the joy ignites,
With quartz that dreams of starry nights.
We gather close, where time aligns,
In rustic love, our heart entwines.

Breath of the Elders in Quiet Tales

In the whisper of the ancient trees,
Tales flutter softly on the breeze.
Roots entwine with stories old,
Secrets of the heart unfold.

Moonlit shadows dance and sway,
Guiding lost souls on their way.
Echoes of forgotten lore,
In twilight's grasp, they softly soar.

Stars peer down from velvet skies,
Holding wishes, dreams, and sighs.
With every breath, the past awakes,
In sacred woods where silence breaks.

Wisdom flows in murmured streams,
Kindling the fire of hidden dreams.
The elders watch with gentle grace,
As night unveils its starry face.

So listen well, O hearts so true,
For in the quiet, magic brews.
In quiet tales, the world shall blend,
With every word, our souls will mend.

Legends Weaved in Celestial Threads

In cosmic looms where stardust gleams,
Legends are stitched with silken dreams.
Galaxies spin in a dance divine,
Chasing the echoes of a fabled line.

Whispers of heroes on the solar winds,
A tapestry where the heart transcends.
Constellations weave the night's embrace,
Uniting worlds in a timeless grace.

Through nebulae, an ardent glow,
Disclosing tales through the ageless flow.
Mysterious paths of celestial grace,
Rising like phoenixes in boundless space.

Legends whisper of fates entwined,
Of shadows that flicker and stars aligned.
Chasing the dreams of those who dare,
To wander realms beyond compare.

In every legend, a flicker remains,
In celestial threads, our spirit gains.
Through endless night, our stories thread,
In the cosmic dance, our lives are bred.

Serenade of the Prowling Dawn

As dawn awakens with gentle grace,
Whispers of light begin to lace.
Over fields where shadows played,
The serenade of day is made.

Crisp air dances with the dew,
Birds join in with songs anew.
In the horizon, colors beam,
Crafting dreams from night's soft seam.

The world unveils in golden hue,
Each blade of grass a vibrant clue.
Nature's melody fills the skies,
As echoes of the night slowly die.

With every step, the creatures stir,
In the quiet, they begin to purr.
Underneath the waking sun,
All of life sings, bound as one.

So breathe in deep this joyful sound,
The serenade of the prowling dawn.
With each new day, a chance to find,
The magic held within the mind.

The Flickering Heart of Nature's Peace

In the silence where the wild things roam,
A flickering heart finds its home.
Amidst the trees and rivers wide,
Nature's peace whispers beside.

A symphony of rustling leaves,
The earth in quietude believes.
Each creature rests in soft embrace,
Finding solace in this sacred space.

Moonlit paths invite the night,
Illuminating hearts with gentle light.
In twilight's grace, the world stands still,
As echoes blend with every thrill.

The stars above, a tender guide,
Lead us on with dreams inside.
In the flickering heart of the trees,
We find our hope, our sweetest ease.

So let us wander where shadows play,
In nature's arms, we'll softly sway.
For in this peace, our spirits leap,
In nature's heart, our dreams we keep.

The Golden Glows of Mountain Katydids

In twilight's hush, the katydids sing,
Their golden glows, a fluttering wing.
Among the whispers of ancient trees,
Nature's pulse flows with every breeze.

The moonlight dances on emerald leaves,
While the world around us gently weaves.
Beneath the stars in a velvet night,
Magic stirs with soft delight.

Each note from the hills is sweet and clear,
Echoing tales for those who hear.
A symphony made of faintest sounds,
In this verdant home, enchantment abounds.

As shadows blend in the forest deep,
The secrets of night our hearts shall keep.
Life's mysteries trace in rhythmic flow,
In golden glows, our dreams shall grow.

Beneath the Guardian's Gaze

The ancient oak stands proud and still,
Guarding the vale with steadfast will.
Beneath its branches, whispers awake,
Stories of time, a woven quake.

In every rustle, the past unfolds,
Of knights and tales that never grow old.
The moonbeams cast a silver hue,
While shadows dance in a secret view.

A tapestry of lives long gone,
Threads of magic by starlight drawn.
In the stillness, dreams take flight,
Beneath the guardian's watchful light.

With each gust, a memory stirs,
Echoes of laughter like gentle purrs.
Each root embraces the secrets told,
In stillness profound, our hearts behold.

Embers of the Nightingale's Nest

Nestled high in a silver tree,
The nightingale sings so soft and free.
Embers glow where the shadows play,
Golden songs mark the end of day.

Wrapped in warmth of dusky light,
With each note, the stars ignite.
Her melodies weave through the air,
Beneath the moon's soft, tender stare.

The nest, a cradle of love and cheer,
Whispers of hope that linger near.
In every flutter, a promise made,
Life's fleeting moments, a gentle cascade.

As twilight deepens, the world takes pause,
Admiring beauty without a cause.
In nightingale's song, hearts find rest,
Embers glow in this sweet, sacred nest.

Mystical Rays over Verdant Peaks

As dawn awakens, the peaks alight,
Mystical rays chase away the night.
Painting the world with colors bright,
In harmony, they bring sheer delight.

The valleys shimmer, the rivers gleam,
Cradled in nature's gentle dream.
Each breeze carries a tale untold,
In whispered tones of the brave and bold.

With every step on the emerald ground,
Mysteries linger, waiting to be found.
A symphony of life in crisp morning air,
Where wonders blossom everywhere.

As sunlight drapes each leaf and stone,
The hearts of wanderers feel at home.
In rays that sparkle on verdant peak,
Nature's language is what we seek.

A Flare of Hope among Ether and Stone

In shadows deep where whispers dwell,
A spark ignites, a tale to tell.
Amidst the gloom, one can perceive,
A beacon bright, we dare believe.

The stars align with gentle grace,
Each heartbeat finds its rightful place.
In every corner, magic stirs,
A song of hope that softly purrs.

Through misty dawn, our spirits rise,
With fiery hues that paint the skies.
The path ahead, though fraught with doubt,
Will guide us forth to what's about.

The stone may hide its timeless lore,
But within each crack, we find much more.
Together we shall face the night,
With every dream, we find our light.

So hold my hand, we'll journey far,
With faith that shines like a distant star.
For in the dance of fate and fate,
A flare of hope will not abate.

Legends Carved in Shimmering Traces

In twilight's grip, the stories flow,
Of heroes brave, their hearts aglow.
Beneath the moon, in whispers sung,
The ancient tales are softly strung.

With ink of stars on parchment bright,
Each stroke reveals a hidden light.
Through mountains vast, and valleys deep,
The legends wake from timeless sleep.

In every shadow, legends gleam,
A tapestry where dreams redeem.
Carved in stone, yet so alive,
In every heart, their spirits thrive.

With laughter light and sorrow's weight,
The tales endure, they navigate.
In shimmering traces, truth unfolds,
As whispers of the brave retold.

So gather round, and heed the call,
For in these tales, we rise, we fall.
Embrace the night, let legends soar,
In shimmering traces, we explore.

The Holy Dance of Lavish Dreams

In meadows bright where wildflowers sway,
A dance unfolds at break of day.
The blossoms twirl, the breezes cheer,
In lavish dreams, we shed our fear.

With every step, the ground we grace,
Awakens joy in time and space.
The sun bequeaths its golden light,
To guide us through the endless night.

With laughter echoing on the air,
We weave our hopes, a vibrant snare.
In visions grand and colors pure,
The holy dance, our dreams endure.

Each heartbeat joins the rhythmic throng,
In harmony, we find our song.
With outstretched arms, we reach for more,
In lavish dreams, our spirits soar.

So let us dance 'neath stars above,
With every twirl, we feel the love.
For in this moment, joys redeem,
Together we create our dream.

Pulse of Life at the Pinnacle's Birth

Atop the peaks where silence reigns,
A pulse of life through vast terrains.
In dawn's embrace, the world awakes,
With every heartbeat, wonder shakes.

The gentle breeze, a tender sigh,
As whispers echo to the sky.
With every step on ancient stone,
The pulse resounds, we're not alone.

In valleys deep and rivers wide,
The life-force flows like a rising tide.
With every heartbeat, dreams ignite,
At pinnacle's birth, we find our light.

So climb with hope, through trials grim,
Each height we reach, we dance, we swim.
In unity, together we strive,
To feel the pulse of life alive.

So heed the call of mountain's song,
In every breath, we all belong.
For at the peak, our spirits blend,
In life's great dance, we transcend.

The Scents of Flourishing High

In valleys deep where flowers bloom,
The air is sweet with nature's plume.
Each petal sways in sunlight's grace,
  A dance of colors, each in place.

Above the hills, the breezes call,
They whisper tales of life for all.
The scents of lavender and pine,
  A tapestry of earth divine.

With every breath, the soul ignites,
In blossoms' chorus, pure delights.
From morning mist to evening's sigh,
The scents of flourishing high will fly.

The buzzing bees, a gentle hum,
With careful craft, their work begun.
In fields of gold, they toil and weave,
A story written by those who believe.

So wander slow through nature's scene,
Embrace the magic, sweet and keen.
In blooming paths, let spirits rise,
The scents of life beneath the skies.

Flickering Glimmers on Nature's Edge

At twilight's door, where shadows play,
A flicker calls the night to stay.
The stars ignite the darkened sea,
Embracing dreams in harmony.

Each glimmer whispers tales of old,
Of treasures found and hearts of gold.
The rustling leaves in gentle breeze,
Dance softly, swaying with such ease.

By riverside, the fireflies glow,
In secret winks, they dance and flow.
Their light a guide, a beacon bright,
That paints the world in silver light.

Upon the cliffs where eagles soar,
Nature unveils her endless lore.
With every spark, a story weaves,
In nature's edge, the heart believes.

So let the flickers light your way,
A symphony of night and day.
In every glimmer, find your peace,
Where nature's wonders never cease.

Flight Beneath the Glistening Stars

Beneath the cloak of velvet night,
The stars awake, a wondrous sight.
With wings unfurled, the dreams take flight,
In whispers soft, we chase the light.

The moon hangs low, a silver guide,
Through paths where silent wishes glide.
Each heartbeat sways with cosmic grace,
In starlit skies, we find our place.

The constellations share their lore,
Of ancient tales and distant shores.
We call to spirits, wild and free,
In every twinkle, a mystery.

As shadows dance, we feel the thrill,
Of journeys taken, hearts that fill.
In the cool breeze, a promise lies,
For those who dare to rise and fly.

So spread your wings, embrace the night,
And let your soul take wondrous flight.
Beneath the stars, the world expands,
In dreams of flight, we take our stand.

Reflections of Joy on Cliffside Wonders

Upon the cliffs, where heights embrace,
The world below unveils its grace.
With every wave, a story swells,
In echoes deep, where nature dwells.

The sunlight dances on the sea,
In playful splashes, wild and free.
Each ripple sings of joyful times,
A symphony of nature's chimes.

Through tangled paths and rocky trails,
We journey forth, where beauty never fails.
With hearts aglow and spirits high,
We find our joy where legends lie.

The whispering winds weave tales of old,
Of wanderers brave, and hearts of gold.
In every step, we seek the thrill,
Reflections spark, the soul to fill.

So let the cliffside wonders call,
With each new dawn, we stand, enthralled.
In nature's arms, our hearts align,
Reflections of joy, forever shine.

A Nest of Dreams and Starlight

In a meadow where shadows play,
Whispers of night softly sway.
Beneath the glow of the crescent moon,
Dreams take flight, sweetly attune.

In the hush of a velvet sky,
Stars weave tales as time drifts by.
Feathers of dusk gently flowing,
Nestled in hopes, the dreams are growing.

A soft breeze hums a tender tune,
Carrying wishes like autumn's boon.
Every flicker, a story untold,
A past that glimmers in silver and gold.

Through the thicket, enchantments roam,
Each breath a note, crafting a home.
In the heart of the night's embrace,
Finding solace in starlight's grace.

As dawn approaches, the dreams take flight,
Leaving echoes of shimmering light.
In the nest where shadows spread,
The stories live, where hopes are fed.

Secrets of the Ancient Crag

Deep in the heart of the echoing stone,
Where whispers linger and winds have blown.
The ancient crag stands tall and proud,
Guarding secrets beneath a shroud.

With every crack and crevice seen,
Time has etched its tale between.
Stones that pulse with a quiet song,
Echoing tales of the ages long.

Glimmers of magic, like stardust, trace,
Stories of old in their hidden grace.
In the shadows where secrets dwell,
The heart of the crag holds their spell.

A riddle wrapped in the earth's embrace,
Calling the brave to its ancient place.
Mysteries whispered on each cold breeze,
Echoing truths that bend the trees.

With every step on the rugged track,
The crag reveals what the past won't lack.
Legends awaken with each new dawn,
In this haven where dreams are drawn.

Glints of Hope Through Mystic Vines

In a grove where the twilight weaves,
Whispers curl like autumn leaves.
Vines of mystery twist and twine,
Cradling dreams in their verdant line.

Each glint of light, a promise made,
A dance of shadows beneath the shade.
Through emerald threads, hope does take flight,
Braiding the day with the softness of night.

Every petal, a wish unfurled,
Petals embracing the hidden world.
In the silence, secrets brew,
A tapestry rich with every hue.

Bravely some wander in search of the true,
Finding the strength that all must pursue.
In the heart of the vines, the magic flows,
Fueling the light when the darkness grows.

The scent of adventure fills the air,
Leading the lost to a realm so rare.
Among the mystic, with hearts aligned,
Glimmers of hope dance in their mind.

The Luminous Arena of the Sky

When twilight falls, the stars ignite,
In a celestial dance, pure and bright.
The arena opens where dreams collide,
Shimmering paths of the cosmic tide.

Each twinkle a spark in the vast expanse,
Inviting souls to join in the dance.
Galaxies swirl, a vibrant hue,
Painting the darkness, a wondrous view.

In this luminous place, fears take flight,
Hearts set free in the cloak of night.
Echoes of laughter and whispers shared,
Binding the brave who have dared.

Above the world where wishes bloom,
Hope is woven through the stillness, a loom.
Every star, a beacon that calls,
Filling the heart as the night gently falls.

As dawn approaches, the light will entwine,
Softening edges of shadows divine.
In the arena where the cosmos stir,
Each soul awakens, as dreams occur.

A Symphony of Golden Echoes

In the dawn's embrace, shadows play,
Whispers of secrets carried away.
Leaves in the wind, a gentle sway,
A symphony weaves, bright as day.

Notes of laughter, crisp and clear,
Dancing on breezes, drawing near.
Harmony wraps the world in cheer,
Golden echoes spark, bring good cheer.

Rays of sunshine glint and gleam,
Chasing the tendrils of a dream.
Nature's chorus, a wild stream,
Flowing with magic, bright and supreme.

Petals in the rush, softly fall,
Caressed by whispers, a tender call.
In the silence, we hear it all,
A symphony sings, and we enthrall.

The Aura of the Feathered Sentinel

In twilight's glow, the sentinel stands,
Wings outstretched, like mystical hands.
Feathers glisten in silver strands,
Guarding the night, with ancient commands.

Eyes like stars, they pierce the dark,
A flicker of hope, a gentle spark.
Guiding lost souls through the stark,
Their presence lingers, a luminous mark.

On velvet nights, the stories unfold,
Of forgotten realms, and legends old.
Each flap of wings, a tale retold,
In the hush of night, so brave, so bold.

Beneath the moon's soft silver light,
The feathered guardian takes to flight.
A watchful heart in the depths of night,
With whispers of wisdom, pure and bright.

Fables Written in Moonlight and Dust

Beneath the stars, in shadows cast,
Fables are born, from memories past.
In moonlit glades, shadows are vast,
Whispering tales in the night's soft blast.

Dust motes dance in silvery beams,
Weaving a tapestry of dreams.
In every sigh, the magic seems,
To echo softly, among the streams.

Ancient voices, a cryptic throng,
Tell of journeys, where hearts belong.
In the stillness, we hear their song,
A melody sweet, both bold and strong.

Each tale a thread that brightly glows,
Binding the past with tomorrow's prose.
In the still of night, the wisdom flows,
Fables ignite where the wild wind blows.

Chasing Dappled Light at Dawn

In the hush of morning, shadows twine,
Dappled light dances, sweet and fine.
Chasing the warmth, a heart divine,
Awakening dreams in the sun's design.

Every petal, a flicker of grace,
Bathed in gold, the world we embrace.
Nature's palette, a vibrant space,
We weave our hopes at an endless pace.

Birdsong rises, a joyful refrain,
Promises linger in the soft rain.
The dawn unfolds, wiping out pain,
In the dappled light, all dreams regain.

With each new step, adventures are found,
In the glow of day, where hopes abound.
Chasing the light, forever unbound,
In the warmth of dawn, our hearts surround.

Mirage of Sweetness in Wild Places

In the heart where whispers play,
Sweet scents of blooms in disarray,
A moment caught, a soft embrace,
Mirage of joy in wildest space.

Among the trees, the shadows sway,
Lives the dream where spirits stray,
Nature's voice, a gentle trace,
Woven threads in time's database.

Golden rays through petals spill,
A tapestry of nature's will,
Each breath, a sip of honeyed grace,
Echoes of laughter weave the place.

In every nook, a story hums,
A symphony of wild drums,
When hearts collide, they interlace,
In mirage found, no need for haste.

So linger here where magic gleams,
In wild places, dance your dreams,
Let sweetness guide, let hope embrace,
In the haven of time and space.

Stars Dripping from Chiseled Crowns

On velvet nights, they softly glow,
Like whispers of the ages' flow,
Each twinkle holds a tale profound,
Stars dripping down from chiseled crowns.

The moonlight weaves a silver thread,
Around the dreams we dare to shed,
A celestial crown, so tightly wound,
With sparkling jewels that spin around.

In moments caught, our wishes rise,
Like fireflies in the darkening skies,
A dance of light, a love unbound,
Stars dripping soft from heavens found.

When shadows chase the light away,
We find our strength, we softly sway,
In cosmic realms where magic's found,
Those stars, they wear their destined crowns.

So let our hearts wander and roam,
In the spaces where the starlight combs,
For in this dance, we're always crowned,
With dreams of fate, forever bound.

The Dance of Petals on Rock Faces

Upon the cliffs where wild winds play,
Petals twirl in a fierce ballet,
Colors burst like whispers loud,
The dance of life, both fierce and proud.

In sun-kissed fields, they take their flight,
With every breeze, a soft delight,
Find solace in the stones, they grace,
A fleeting touch in nature's space.

As shadows lean on rugged stone,
The petals weave, they dance alone,
In laughter shared, despite the trace,
Of time that leaves a gentle space.

Amidst the crevices, they bloom,
Defying fate, dispelling gloom,
So fierce their joy, in wild embrace,
The dance of petals finds its place.

Let us too, like petals, dare,
To sway and twirl in open air,
For in each step, in every race,
We find our strength in nature's grace.

Twilight's Glint on the Ridge

As day surrenders to night's embrace,
Twilight glints on the mountain's face,
Echoes of dreams in softest sighs,
In shadowed valleys, our spirit flies.

The horizon bleeds with hues of gold,
Tales of the mountains forever told,
Each heartbeat, a whisper, each glance, a bridge,
In the twilight's glint, we find our ridge.

Stars awaken, one by one,
As night blankets the day's weary run,
In whispered winds, our fears are ridged,
A moment cherished on twilight's edge.

Through winding paths where shadows blend,
Hope finds a way, on hearts to mend,
Each step a promise, a gentle pledge,
At the twinkling glow on the evening's ledge.

So gather close, let spirits rise,
In the twilight glow, where magic lies,
With every heartbeat, life will smidge,
In the beauty found on the ridge.

Revelry of the Twilight Keepers

In the hush of dusk, they gather near,
Twilight Keepers, with hearts sincere.
Their laughter echoes through the trees,
As night unfurls, dancing on the breeze.

Candles flicker, casting long shadows,
Whispers of secrets in the glades that follow.
Mirth soars high, where starlight gleams,
And dreams awaken in shimmering streams.

With every twirl, the world grows bright,
Gracing the wild with pure delight.
Fairies flit in a playful game,
While gentle moons ignite their flame.

They spin like leaves in a silken wind,
A symphony of joy, where hopes rescind.
In unity, their spirits meld,
In the calm embrace of the night upheld.

As dawn approaches, the dance draws near,
But memories linger, forever dear.
For in their revelry, one would find,
A magic woven, beautifully entwined.

The Guardian's Dance of Timelessness

In the heart of stillness, wisdom twirls,
A Guardian awaits, as time unfurls.
With every step, moments replay,
In the dance of the ages, night meets day.

Veils of time, like ribbons of gold,
Spun by hands both gentle and bold.
Echoes of laughter, whispers of woes,
In this hallowed ground, true love grows.

The moon bathes the earth in a silvery hue,
Casting shadows, where dreams come true.
Guardian's watch, in silence profound,
Marking the rhythm of life's sacred sound.

Through the ages, the dance shall weave,
Stories of hearts that dare believe.
In the tapestry woven, a truth so bright,
Time expands, in the soft twilight.

As stars begin to fade from view,
The Guardian bows, as if it knew.
In this moment, the dance stands still,
As time's gentle hand writes its will.

Enchantment Where Shadows Dare

In a forest deep where shadows play,
Mysteries linger, night turns to day.
Whispers of magic stir the air,
An enchantment blooms, where few would dare.

Glimmers of light through branches weave,
Secrets hiding, waiting to believe.
Footsteps lead to hidden glades,
Where visions dance and dreams parade.

The moon smiles down with a knowing gleam,
As shadows whisper their midnight theme.
Lost in the rhythm of the earth's own heart,
An adventure awaits, a wondrous start.

With every breath, the world unfurls,
Painting a canvas of ancient swirls.
Here, the bold and the timid blend,
In enchantment's embrace, where fears suspend.

As dawn peeks in, the magic stays,
In the gentle light of fading ways.
For those who crave more than what is bare,
Find solace in enchantment, where shadows dare.

Luminary Tales at the Cliff's Edge

On the precipice where the wild winds sigh,
Luminaries gather, casting dreams high.
Each tale a spark, a flickering flame,
Illuminating paths, none are the same.

With hearts unbound, they share their lore,
Whispers of magic from ages before.
The ocean's roar beneath them sings,
As starlight dances on moonlit wings.

From gallant knights to fair maidens fair,
Adventures unfold, woven with care.
Inspiration taken from night's embrace,
Each story is cradled in warm grace.

The cliffs stand tall, a guardian true,
Holding their secrets, as if they knew.
And as the tide draws closer still,
The tales inspire a heart to fill.

As dawn breaks soft on the horizon wide,
Stories linger, with the ocean's tide.
For in those moments at the cliff's edge,
Luminary tales forever pledge.